BOBBIN LACE PATTERNS

*37 patterns
with
tear-out prickings*

Tiny Zwaal-Lint

Foreword by Pamela Nottingham

B. T. Batsford Ltd, London

© Cantecleer bv, de Bilt, 1981
First published in English 1984, by
B. T. Batsford Ltd,
4 Fitzhardinge Street,
London, W1H 0AH

ISBN 0 7134 4442 8

Printed in the Netherlands

This book of lace patterns from Holland has variety and several attractive techniques rarely seen elsewhere; for example, the use of thick, soft weaver threads in pattern 5, the unusual ground in torchon patterns 11, 12 and 22, and the shaped lampshade panel in 21.

For those lacemakers who prefer to work in finer threads, reduction copying is readily available and many of the edgings and mats are particularly attractive on a smaller scale.

The superb photographs and diagrams give clear indication of the working methods. At first sight, the prickings may appear incomplete, but it is usual practice to leave some holes to be put in by the worker.

Patterns with outline trails leave the positioning of holes at the discretion of the lacemaker. With reference to the photographs it is possible to draw in the path of the weaver, taking care to link it with plaits, leaves or other stitches. Holes can be placed exactly where required and the trails worked easily. In the torchon patterns the position of holes is indicated by the guide lines.

The availability of well-marked ready-to-use patterns with accompanying photographs allows the lacemaker to escape from the difficult and tedious task of preparing prickings. This is a worthwhile addition to any lacemaker's collection of books.

Introduction

Recently interest in the art of bobbin lacemaking has grown enormously. This is fortunate, for it has always been one of the finest expressions of needlecraft. More and more women — and occasionally men too — are taking lessons and forming lace groups. Books have been published in which the basic elements are clearly described, and more and more space is devoted to this splendid and fascinating craft in needlework magazines.

This book is not a repetition of what is already available. It should be seen, rather, as a continuation, or an addition, filling a gap which still seems to exist. It seeks to give an answer to the often-heard question: 'Where can I find patterns with sufficient information to enable me to make them myself?'

Hence this book of patterns. It assumes that you have mastered the technicalities of bobbin lacemaking and that you know how to make the stitches, although they are dealt with briefly in the introductory section—

perhaps needlessly. Additionally, this book tries to offer you some help in starting off each piece of lace.

The patterns, each of them designed by the author herself, provide a variety of lace work, from simple laces to intricate ones. The way they are selected will enable you to use them in various ways; the frontispiece shows one such suggestion. They are not meant to be stored away in a cupboard, or to be shown in a plastic folder; you can actually use them! Experienced lacemakers will notice that I have taken the liberty of applying different techniques in one and the same pattern.

I hope that through this book many may find the inspiration to progress with this beautiful hobby and that others may take the opportunity to make a start with it.

Bobbin lacemaking is worth it!

Some introductory remarks

For each pattern in this book you will find:
— A photograph of the piece of lace, or part of it, shown actual size. This photograph shows the upper side of the lace, the side which faces the pillow while working the pattern. For the sake of clarity you will often find an enlargement of a detail. This enlargement shows the underside, i.e. the side you see while making the lace. (You will find these photographs in the first part of the book).
— Next to that, in the first part of the book, are given: the setting-up diagram, the required number of bobbins, the thickness of the thread and a brief description of the working method.
— The latter part of the book consists of the prickings,

printed on stiffened paper. These prickings can be torn out along the perforations, after which they are ready to be used on the pillow.
If you want to keep the book intact, you can trace the pattern off using transparent paper. This should always be done in ink, not in pencil, as pencil will rub off and make the work dirty. The pricking achieved in this way is stuck on thin cardboard at the corners.
— Some of the prickings could not be placed on one page and were therefore spread over two. If you place the asterisks printed at the side of these prickings exactly on top of each other, you will have your pattern complete.

All patterns were worked with BOUC linen thread, so the thread thicknesses mentioned match their numbering. These are equivalent to the DMC numbers, with which most English lacemakers should be familiar. Of course, other linen threads can be used as well.
Cotton threads are not recommended. These are too resilient, which makes the work less beautiful.
An exception are the gimps used in some of the patterns. For these MEZ Perlgarn was invariably used, but any other thick cotton thread will do.
If you like, the gimps of which some of the fans are made can be replaced by thread of the same thickness as that used for the lace itself.
The quantity of thread necessary to make the lace is about three-and-a-half times the length or the outline of the lace per bobbin. A pair of bobbins that remain as workers throughout the lace, or a pattern with many leaves, however, requires double the amount of thread.
If a gimp is worked in the pattern, always use a full bobbin. This way you are certain to have enough thread, as it is difficult to start a new gimp neatly. Later in the introduction I show what to do when you run out of thread or when the thread breaks.
If you want to use coloured thread, either bought or dyed yourself, you should always check first whether the dye will run, by means of a sample. To try this out put the sample on a piece of white cloth and iron it with a

steam iron. The cloth should not take on any colour.
If only part of the pattern is available, as is often the case with larger pieces of lace, you will have to move the lace on the pillow. In order to do this you first secure the bobbins by means of a piece of buttonhole elastic or with a crochet braid with holes. If you put a bobbin into each hole, they will not get entangled. Next the pins are removed, and you then carefully move the lace with one hand and the bobbins with the other to their correct positions again.
Edgings and insertions must be pre-shrunk before they are mounted. Moisten the lace with a steam iron and after that iron it till it is dry. It usually turns out to have shrunk about 5 cm to the metre. However, when you want to make an insertion of a certain length it would be wise to allow for a shrinkage of 10%.
With mats a very fine result is achieved by proceeding as follows: put the working diagram you have been using onto a piece of soft board and cover this with a sheet of transparent plastic. Fit the lace tightly to the diagram with pins. Apply some starch, e.g. a spray textile starch. When it is dry remove the pins.

Finally, I have given a short description of the stitches and working methods used in the patterns.

And after all these hints, lots of success with the work!

Half stitch (4 bobbins)

Cross-twist

Whole stitch and twist (4 bobbins)

Cross-twist
Cross-twist

Whole stitch (4 bobbins)

Cross-twist-cross

Introducing a gimp (3 bobbins)

Twist the first pair the gimp is to cross. Pass the gimps between the threads and twist again.

Footside stitch (e.g. 3 or 4 pairs of bobbins)
Whole stitch and twist – once or twice whole stitch, or whole stitch and twist, pin between 2nd and 3rd pair. The first pair is not worked.

Torchon ground (2 pairs of bobbins)
Half stitch – pin – half stitch

Spider

Is often worked with 6 pairs of bobbins, 3 left-hand pairs and 3 right-hand pairs. Work the right-hand pairs through the left-hand pairs in whole stitch, pin and back again.

Crossing of plaits (4 pairs of bobbins)

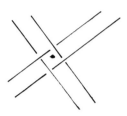

Work the 2 left-hand pairs through the 2 right-hand pairs in whole stitch.
Use 2 bobbins as a single one.
Method:
Cross – twist – pin in centre and then cross.

Leaves (petals) (4 bobbins)

Hold 3 bobbins tightly in your left hand. Weave back and forth with your right hand.
Start with a tight top.

Tallies (4 bobbins)

Worked like leaves, but the threads form straight lines.
If necessary use support pins.

Plaits (2 pairs of bobbins)
Half stitch × 3, pull firmly.
If necessary, half stitch × 4, 5 or 6.

Lille ground or Tulle ground (2 pairs of bobbins)
Half stitch, extra twist, pin.
Do not cover the pin.

Torchon double ground (2 pairs of bobbins)
Whole stitch and twist, pin, whole stitch and twist.

Starting a new thread

When a bobbin runs out of thread or when the thread breaks you can simply and neatly start a new one by proceeding as follows:
- Leave about 20 cm (8 in) of the old thread.
- Wind the new thread onto a bobbin, leaving about 30 cm (12 in)

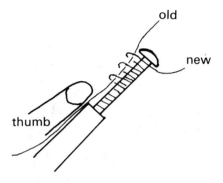

- Bring the old thread to lie alongside the bobbin with the new thread and hold it with the thumb of your left hand (see illustration).
- Wind some 15 cm (6 in) more of the new thread round the bobbin together with the old thread.
- After that secure the new thread with a knot to a pin outside the work.
- Bring the bobbin with the new thread to the same level as the others.
- Now continue making the lace. When the old thread is worked together with the new one for a while, it can be taken off the bobbin. Put the remaining thread upwards on the lace.
- Later on the two threads can be cut off close to the work.

Counting

The counting of the pairs is always from left to right in this book. When an exception to this rule is made, it is clearly indicated in the text.

Triangular ground

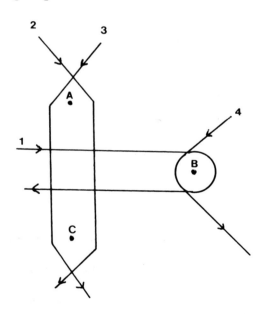

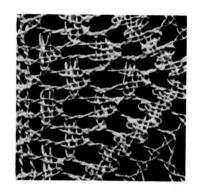

- The pinholes A-B-C form the triangle.
- Triangular ground is worked in whole stitch with 4 pairs of bobbins.
  Twist all 4 pairs to start.
- Whole stitch 2nd and 3rd pair. Pin at A. Do *not* cover the pin.
- Whole stitch 1st pair through 2nd, 3rd and 4th pair. Pin at B and back through 4th, 3rd and 2nd pair. No pin.
- Next a pin at C between 2nd and 3rd pair, whole stitch and twist, etc.

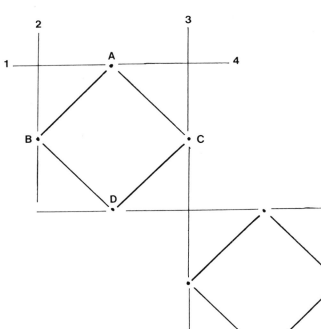

Rose ground

Rose ground is worked with 4 pairs of bobbins:
- Half stitch with 1st and 2nd pair, no pin.
- Half stitch with 3rd and 4th pair, no pin.
- At A 2nd and 3rd pair, half stitch, pin, half stitch.
- At B 1st and 2nd pair, half stitch, pin, half stitch.
- At C 3rd and 4th pair, half stitch, pin, half stitch.
- At D 2nd and 3rd pair, half stitch, pin, half stitch.
- Half stitch with 1st and 2nd pair, no pin.
- Half stitch with 3rd and 4th pair, no pin.
- Begin again at A.

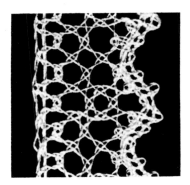

Honeycomb (6 pairs of bobbins)

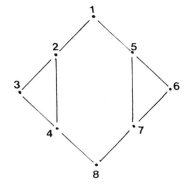

Work half stitch, pin, half stitch in indicated order.

Bias ground (4 pairs of bobbins)

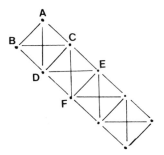

Start with half stitch (intervening stitch).
A and B half stitch, pin, half stitch, with middle pairs half stitch, no pin.
C and D half stitch, pin, half stitch. Intervening half stitch.
E and F half stitch, pin, half stitch. Intervening half stitch, etc.

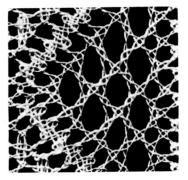

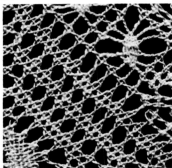

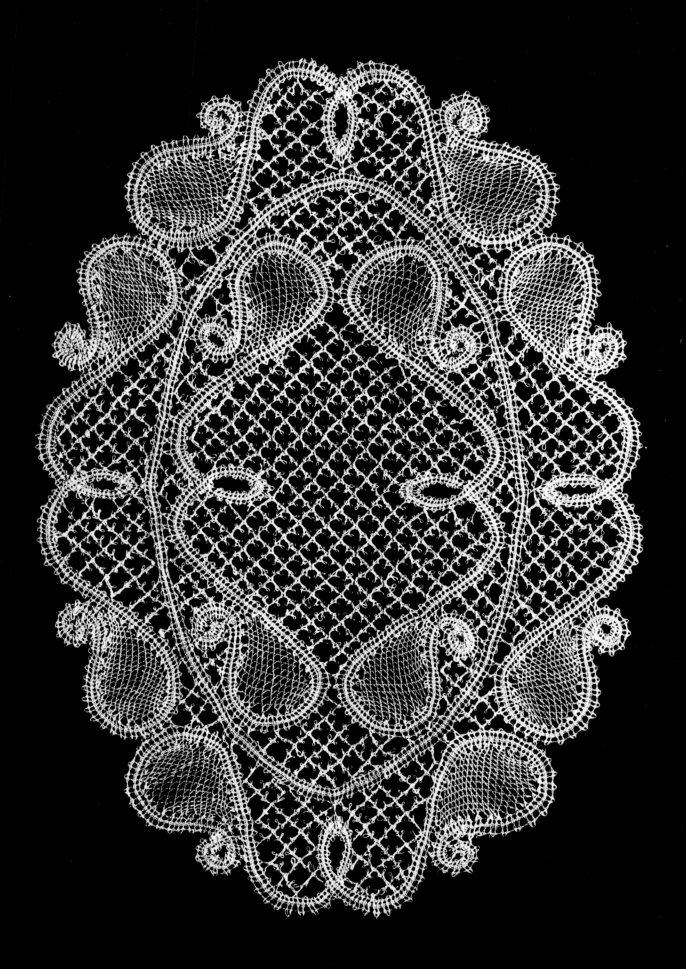

Materials:
- 5 pairs of bobbins for the braids.
- About 11 pairs of bobbins for the half stitch filling in the outer edge.
- About 8 pairs of bobbins for the half stitch filling in the centre.
- About 30 pairs of bobbins for the centre filling made of plaits with picots.
- Thread no. 100.

Working method:
- See pricking.
- Start all braids at A.
- They are worked in whole stitch and twist, 2 whole stitches and whole stitch and twist.
- Sew at the curves.
- Fill the circles with half stitch.
- The other fillings are plaits with picots as indicated on the pricking.

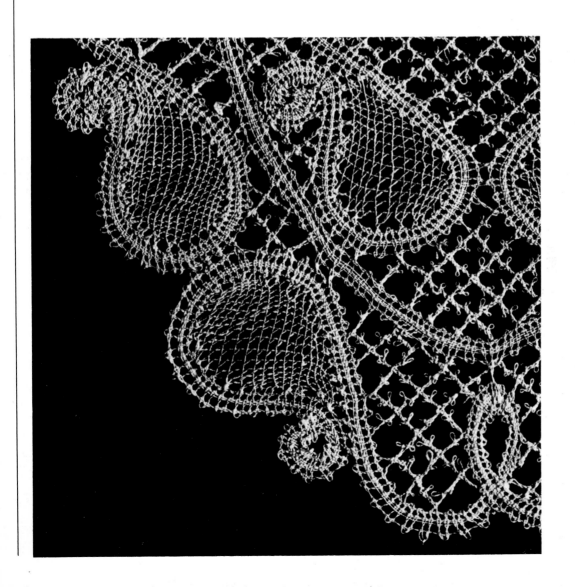

Setting-up diagram

Materials:
- 12 pairs of bobbins with thread no. 70.
- 1 single bobbin with a gimp thread.

Working method:
- Hang the bobbins on the pins as shown in the setting-up diagram.
- At A, 2nd and 3rd pair start torchon ground triangle, working footside stitch, pin, footside stitch.
- with 1st and 2nd pair twisted stitch, *no* pin. In this way a stronger footside is achieved.
- Continue the triangle with 3rd and 4th pair, etc.
- At B hang 2 pairs with thread no. 70 and a single bobbin with a gimp.
- Though used as a worker, the single bobbin should be used as a gimp.

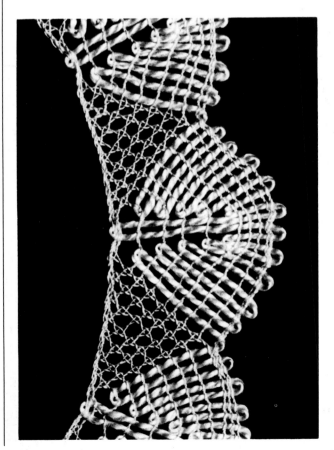

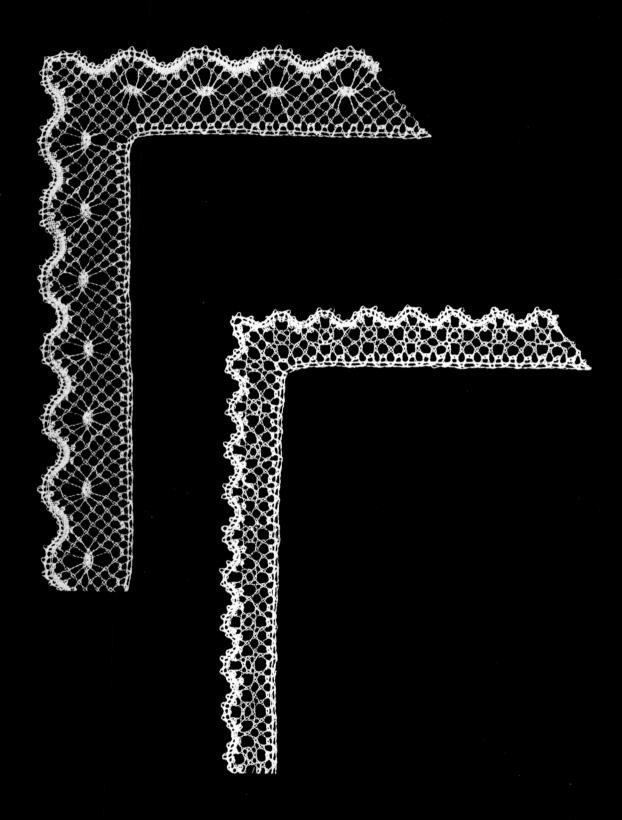

Setting-up diagram

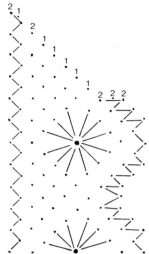

Materials:
— 16 pairs of bobbins.
— Thread no. 80.

Working method:
— Hang the pairs round the pins as shown in the setting-up diagram.
— Stitches used:
  ● footside stitch
  ● torchon ground
  ● spider
  ● for the headside: whole stitch and whole stitch and twist.

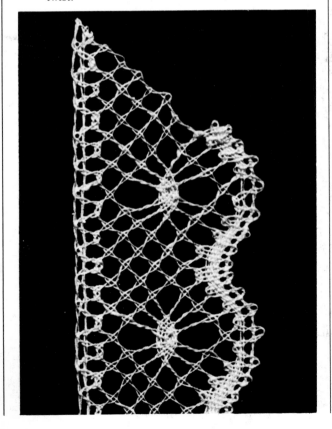

Setting-up diagram

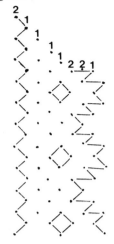

Materials:
— 11 pairs of bobbins.
— Thread no. 80.

Working method:
— Hang on the pairs in accordance with the setting-up diagram.
— Stitches used:
  ● footside stitch
  ● torchon ground
  ● rose ground
  ● headside: whole stitch and whole stitch and twist.

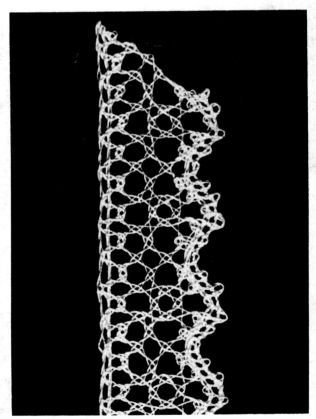

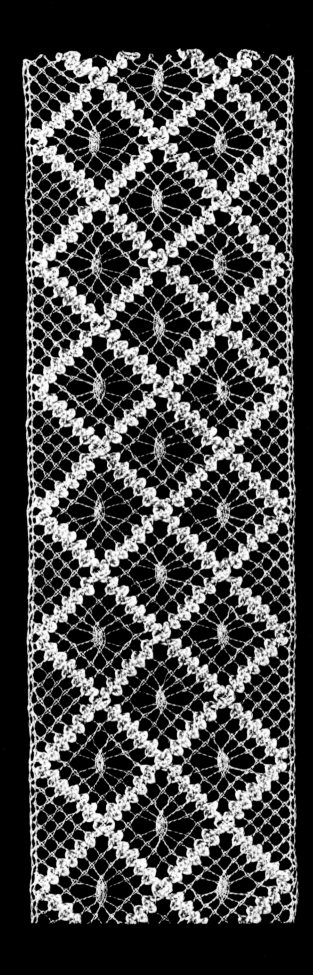

Setting-up diagram

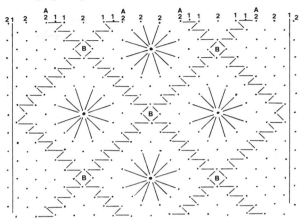

Materials:
- 30 pairs of bobbins with thread no. 30.
- 4 pairs of bobbins with gimp thread, e.g. Mez Perlgarn.

Working method:
- Start as shown in the setting-up diagram.
- At A the gimps are introduced as workers.
- At B cross 4 pairs in whole stitch.
- At both edges: footside stitch, whole stitch and twist, whole stitch with the pair leaving the ground, and half stitch, pin, half stitch.
- Take the left-hand pair from the ground, whole stitch × 1, whole stitch and twist, pin between 2nd and 3rd pair.
- Whole stitch 2nd and 3rd pair and work another pair from the ground, half stitch, pin, half stitch.

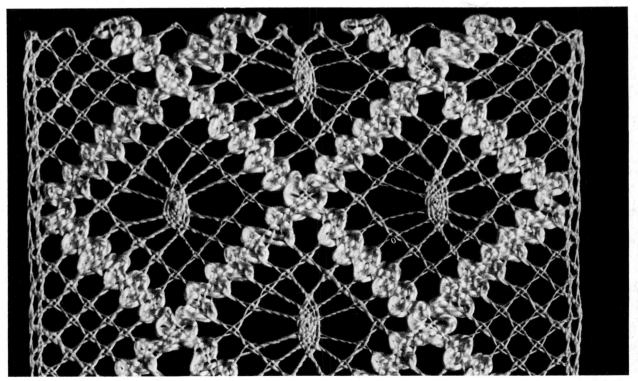

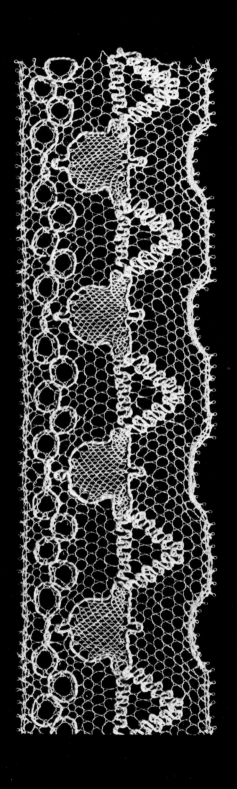

Setting-up diagram

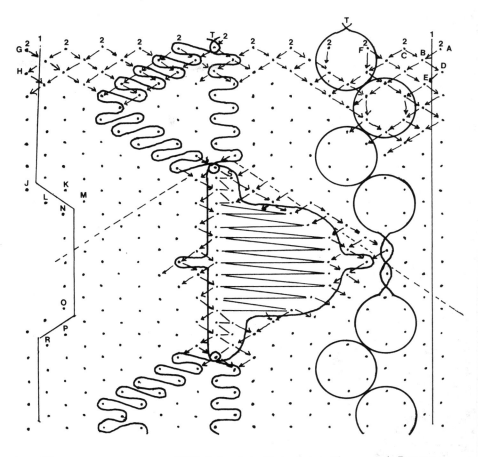

Materials:
- 26 pairs of bobbins with thread no. 80.
- 2 pairs of bobbins with gimp thread.
- 2 pairs of bobbins, thread no. 80, to be introduced at the bell.

Working method:
- Hang the gimp pairs at T, the other pairs as shown in the setting-up diagram.
- The ground of this lace is worked in Bucks point. Bucks point is: half stitch, twist × 2, pin. Do not cover the pin.
- To make the footside, start at A with whole stitch and twist, go to B in whole stitch, pin and twist × 2.
- From C to B with half stitch, twist × 2 (using pinhole B twice), work to D.
- Back to E, put a pin and wait for the pair that is to come from F, etc.
- The honeycomb rings and the garlands are worked half stitch, pin, half stitch, with an extra twist.
- At G picot, twist × 1, whole stitch through heading, twist × 2 and work Bucks point net. Work back whole stitch through heading and picot at H.
- Continue working to J.
- At J picot, whole stitch and twist, whole stitch × 2 and pin at K.
- At L picot, whole stitch and twist, whole stitch × 3 and pin at M.
  From N to O.
- With 4th pair to P, back into the ground.

- With 3rd pair to R, back into the ground. Repeat from G onwards.

Bell
- Hang 2 extra pairs at pinhole S; one is the worker in the bell, the other a passive pair. Work half stitch throughout, pick up 1 pair from the ground every other time and work it back into the ground as indicated by the arrows.
- Take out the 2 added pairs when the bell is finished.

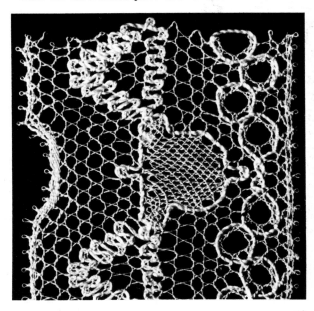

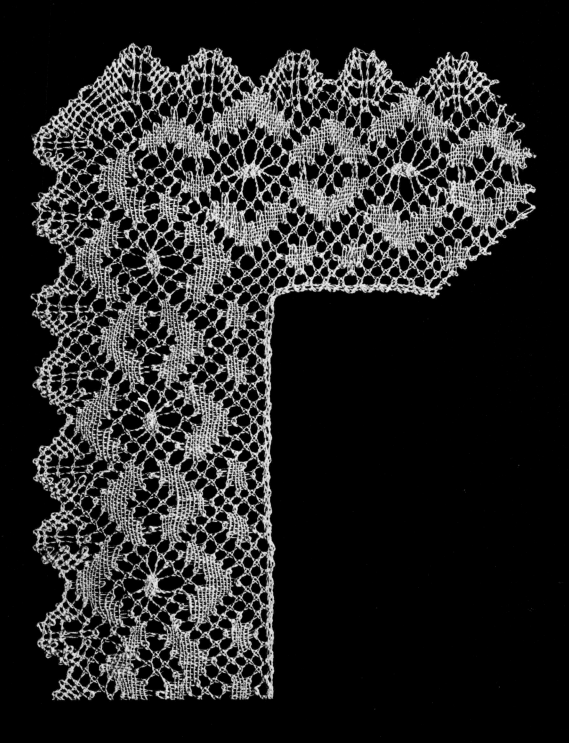

Setting-up diagram

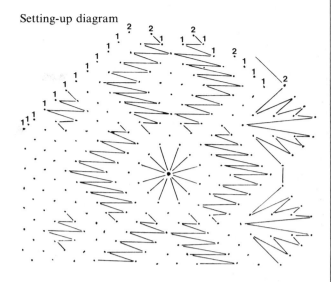

Materials:
− 28 pairs of bobbins.
− Thread no. 40.

Working method
− Hang on the bobbins as shown in the setting-up diagram.
− Stitches used:
  • footside stitch
  • torchon ground
  • whole stitch for diamonds and hearts
  • spider
  • fan in whole stitch and twist

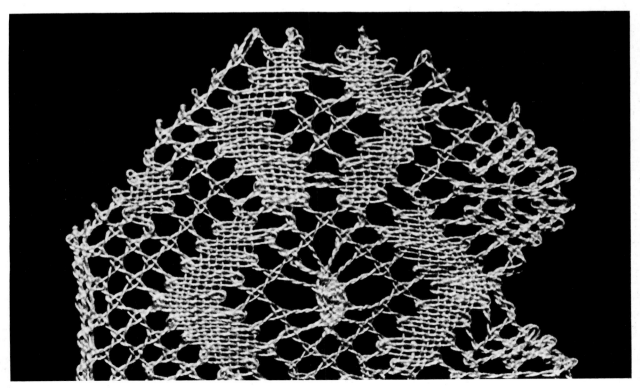

Setting-up diagram A

Setting-up diagram B

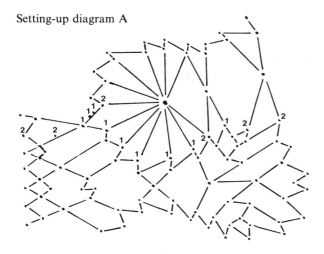

Materials:
- 21 pairs of bobbins for the outer edge.
- About 28 pairs of bobbins for the filling.
- Thread no. 70.

Working method:
- Hang on the bobbins as shown in setting-up diagram A.
- Continue in accordance with setting-up diagram B.
- Start at A, in whole stitch up to D, whole stitch to E, back to F, proceed to G. Continue working this braid to H, either picking up or leaving out pairs.

- At J whole stitch and twist to L.
- Take 1 pair from D, twist × 1 and then to K, whole stitch × 2 with a twist in between.
- At L half stitch, pin, half stitch and at M whole stitch and twist.
- From L to N whole stitch × 2, twist in between.
- At O half stitch, pin, half stitch.
- Continuously repeat the working from K to O.
- The little diamond at P is worked in whole stitch × 4. Spider and half stitch diamond are made with 6 pairs of bobbins leaving and entering the braid.
- The filling is worked as follows: whole stitch and twist, pin, whole stitch and twist × 2.

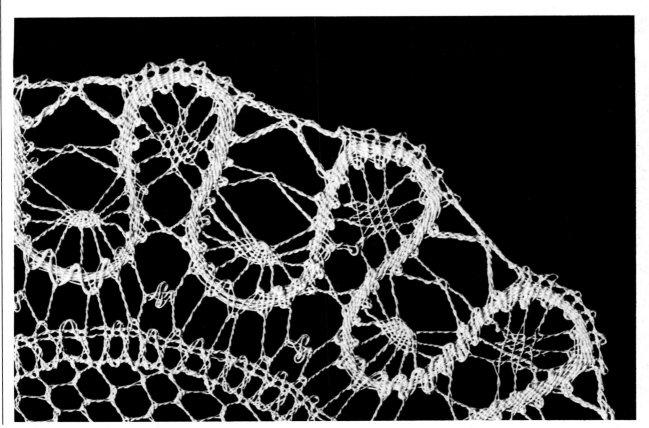

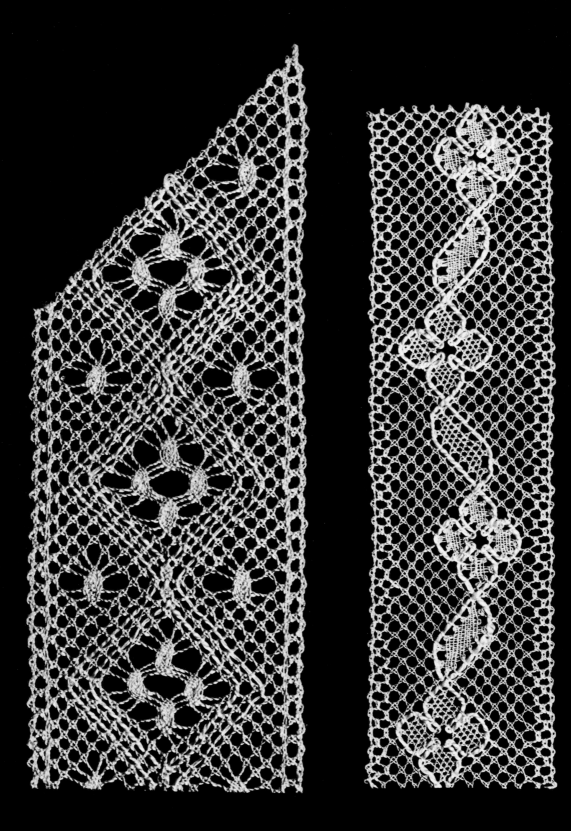

Setting-up diagram

Setting-up diagram

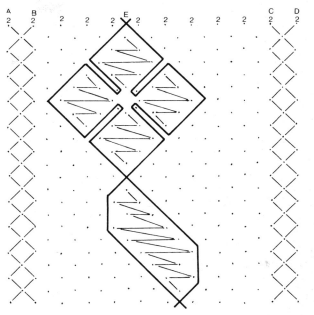

Materials:
- 30 pairs of bobbins, thread no. 20.
- 2 pairs with a gimp.

Working method:
- Hang on the pairs as indicated in the setting-up diagram. The 2 gimp pairs are hung at pinhole D.
- At A whole stitch and twist, the next pair half stitch, pin, half stitch.
- Pass through 3rd pair in whole stitch.
- The net is worked in torchon ground.
- The gimp is passed between the stitches of the ground.
- The square sections in the centre are filled with spiders. No stitch between the spiders.

Materials:
- 24 pairs of bobbins, thread no. 60.
- 1 pair of bobbins with a gimp or other thread (e.g. coloured).

Working method:
- Hang on 2 pairs at A-B and C-D. These pairs are worked whole stitch and twist, pin, whole stitch and twist. They form the edges of the lace.
- The other pairs are worked half stitch, pin, half stitch; the motif is made of whole stitch and half stitch.
- At E the motif is emphasised by a gimp or other thread.

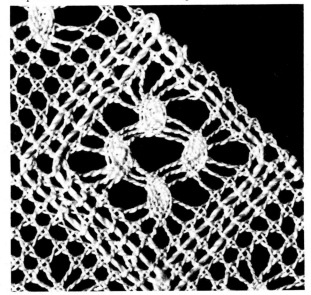

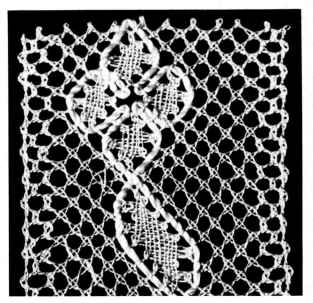

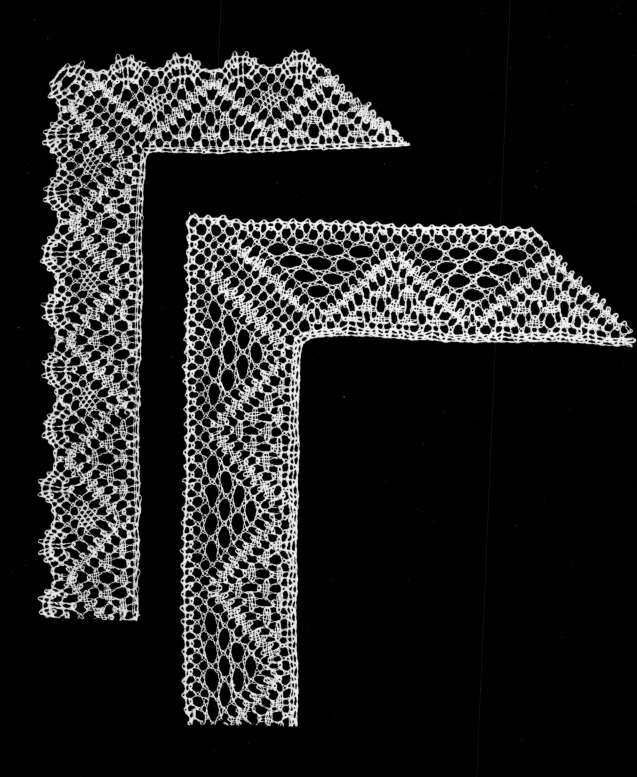

Setting-up diagram

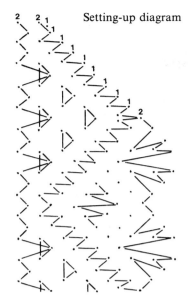

Setting-up diagram

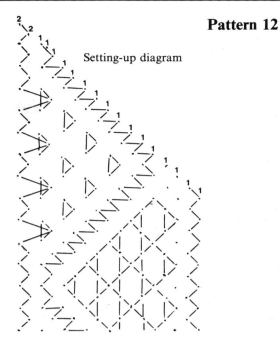

Materials:
- 15 pairs of bobbins.
- Thread no. 70.

Working method:
- Hang on the pairs in accordance with the setting-up diagram.
- Stitches used:
  - footside stitch
  - half stitch, pin, half stitch
  - triangular ground
  - diamond: half stitch
  - fan: twisted stitch

Materials:
- 20 pairs of bobbins.
- Thread no. 70.

Working method:
- Hang on the pairs in accordance with the setting-up diagram.
- Stitches used:
  - footside stitch
  - trail: whole stitch
  - triangular ground
  - honeycomb net

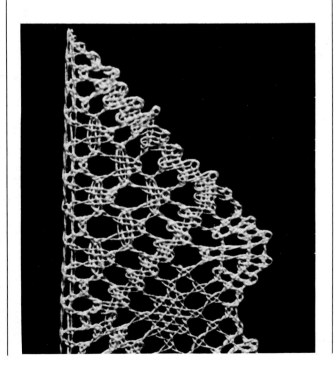

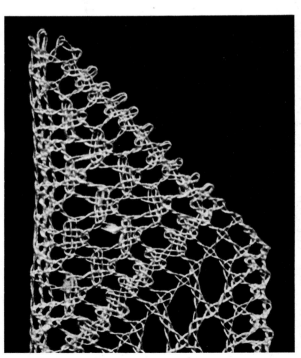

1st setting-up diagram

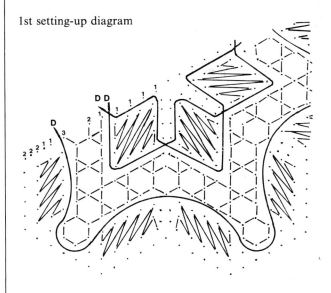

2nd setting-up diagram

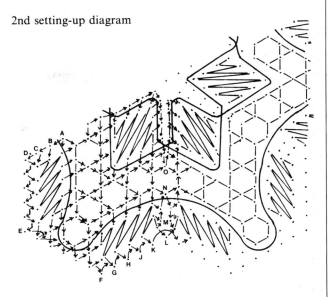

Materials:
- 18 pairs of bobbins, thread no. 40.
- 1 pair of bobbins with a gimp.
- 1 single bobbin with a gimp.

Working method:
- Hang on the pairs as shown in the first setting-up diagram: the single bobbin with gimp thread at D, the gimp pair at DD.
- Now continue as shown in the 2nd setting-up diagram.
- Start at A, whole stitch to D, whole stitch × 5 back.
- Start the rectangle with 7th and 8th pair.
- With 6th pair whole stitch × 3 to the left, picot and return to rectangle.
- Whole stitch × 4 with 5th pair, picot and back into the rectangle.
- Continue this procedure till 2 pairs are left at E.
- Weave 2nd pair in whole stitch through 1st pair, picot and whole stitch back.
- Whole stitch × 2 with 3rd pair, picot and back.
- 3rd and 4th pair half stitch, pin, half stitch.
- 2 × whole stitch with 3rd pair, picot and back.

- Now continue at A; the arrows show the direction of the threads.
- At F, 2nd pair whole stitch, picot and back, no pin.
- At G, 3rd pair whole stitch × 2, picot and back, no pin.
- At H, 4th pair whole stitch × 3, picot and back, no pin.
- At J, 5th pair whole stitch × 4, picot and back, no pin.
- At K, 6th pair whole stitch × 5, picot and back, no pin.
- At L, 7th pair whole stitch × 6, picot and back. This pair enters the rectangle again.
- At M work back and forth as shown by the arrows. This pair enters the rectangle too.
- At N and O whole stitch.
- Recommence with 7th pair, etc. Continue working as described above.

- Now look at the pricking.
- Work the pair coming from P to R, twist several times, pin and at S half stitch, pin, half stitch.
- Proceed to T, working as shown by the arrows.
- Next work the bottom corner till you reach pinhole T again.
  Sew at T as shown by the arrows.

Materials:
- 23 pairs of bobbins.
- Thread no. 60.

Working method:
- Hang the bobbins round the pins as shown in the setting-up diagram.
- At the footside 4 pairs are used for the edge in whole stitch and twist.
- The bias ground is worked in accordance with the illustration next to the setting-up diagram.
  - A and B half stitch, pin, half stitch, with middle pairs half stitch, no pin.
  - C and D half stitch, pin, half stitch, followed by half stitch with the middle pairs, no pin.
  - E and F half stitch, pin, half stitch, middle pairs half stitch, no pin, etc.
  - always finish the row.
- fan in whole stitch and twist.

Setting-up diagram   Detail of bias ground

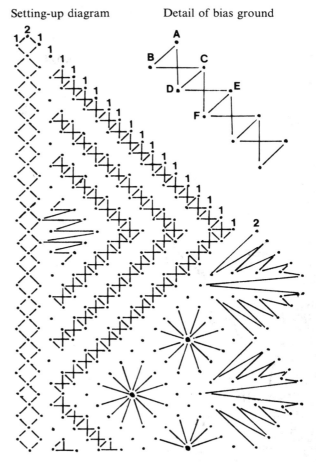

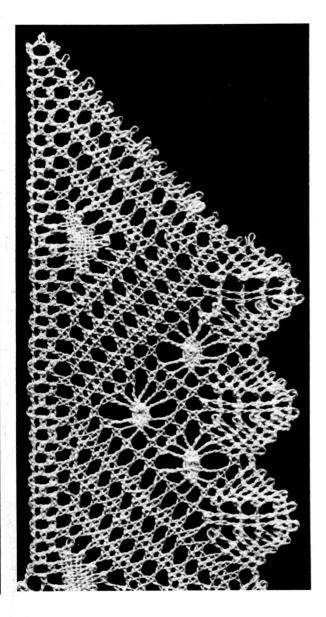

Detail A

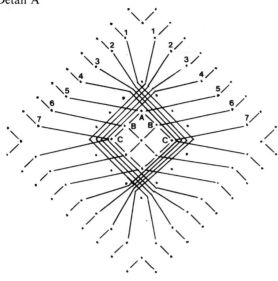

Detail B

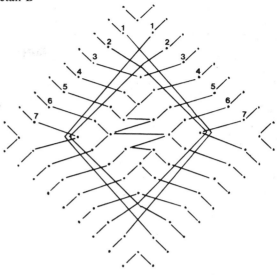

Materials:
- 44 pairs of bobbins with thread no. 40.
- 1 pair of bobbins with a gimp.

Working method:
- Hang the pairs round the pins as shown in the pricking. Gimp at D.
- For this piece of lace the following stitches were used:
  - footside stitch
  - whole stitch
  - triangular ground
  - torchon double ground
  - open spiders with variations
  These motifs are worked as shown in the detailed drawings.

A. To start the top of the open spider weave 4 left hand pairs through 4 right hand pairs in whole stitch. Whole stitch pairs nos. 5 to pinhole A. Whole stitch pairs nos. 6 to B. Whole stitch pairs nos. 7 to C; after torchon double ground they leave the spider again. Bring the pairs to their correct positions in reverse direction. If necessary, support pins can be put along the outline of the spider to keep it in shape.

B. Whole stitch 2 left hand pairs through 2 right hand pairs to start the top of the spider. These 2 pairs are passed through the next 5 pairs as gimps. Work the centre motif in torchon double ground and whole stitch and bring the pairs to their correct positions again.

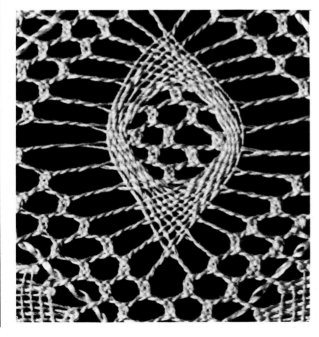

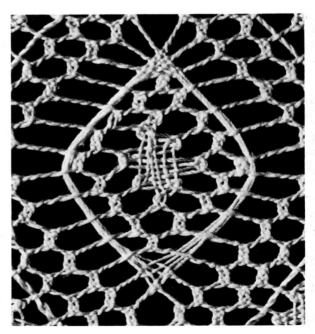

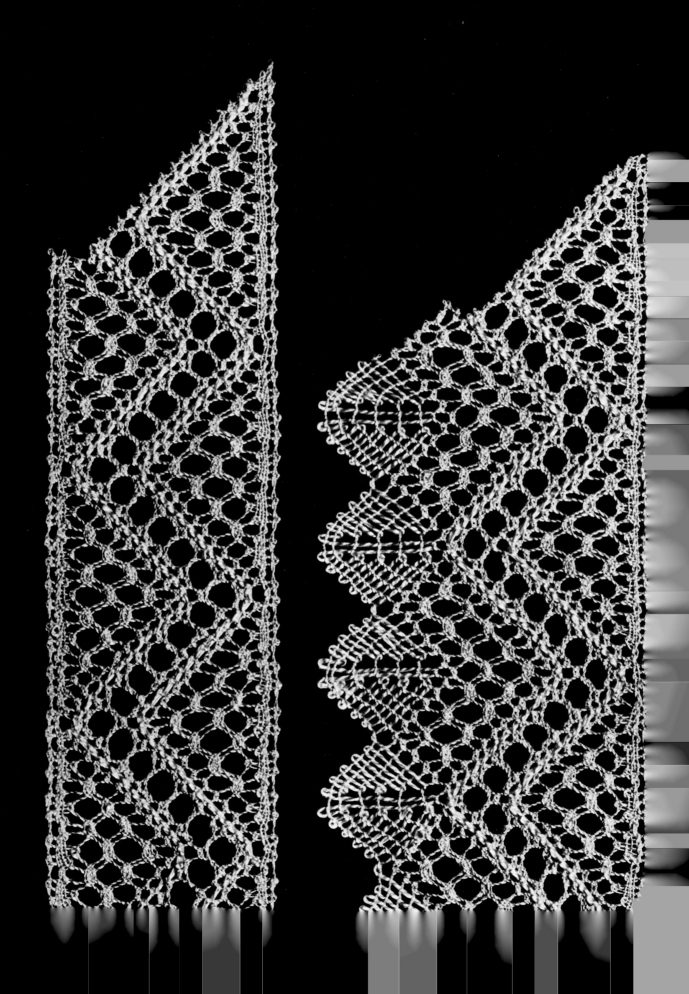

Pattern 16

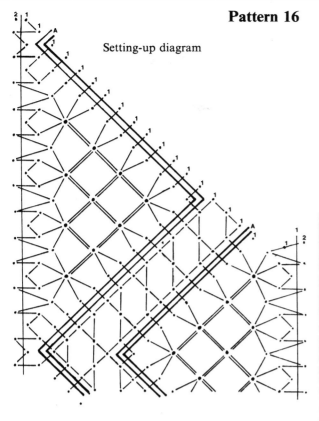

Setting-up diagram

Pattern 17

Setting-up diagram

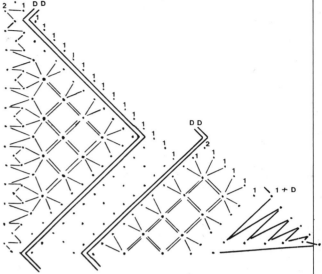

Materials:
- 24 pairs of bobbins, thread no. 20.
- 2 pairs of bobbins with a gimp, or other thread, e.g. coloured.

Working method:
- Hang the bobbins on the pins as shown in the setting-up diagram.
- The pattern is worked in spiders and 'honeycomb' stitches.
- The zig-zag made of 'honeycomb' is worked whole stitch and twist, pin, whole stitch and twist (in fact, torchon double ground).
- The gimp is hung at A, 1 pair × 2.
- The gimp is whole stitched between the torchon double ground.

Materials:
- 28 pairs of bobbins, thread no. 20.
- 2 pairs of gimps.
- 1 single bobbin with a gimp thread.

Working method:
- Hang the bobbins on the pins as shown in the setting-up diagram.
  The gimp pairs are hung at DD, the single bobbin with gimp thread at D.
- This pattern is a variation of pattern no. 16, so for working look at that pattern as well.
- The fan is made with the gimp thread used as worker.

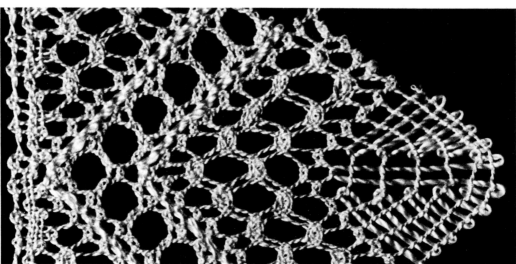

Setting-up diagram

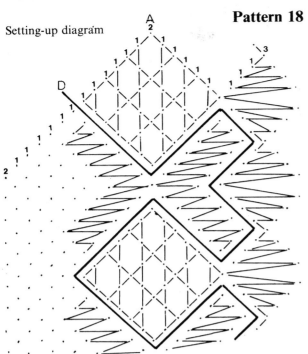

Materials:
- 27 pairs of bobbins, thread no. 80.
- 1 bobbin with a gimp.

Working method:
- Hang the pairs round the pins as shown in the setting-up diagram.
- The gimp is hung at D.
- Start at A.
- The stitches used are:
  - honeycomb net
  - whole stitch
  - torchon ground
  - footside stitch
  - connection: whole stitch, pin, whole stitch and twist

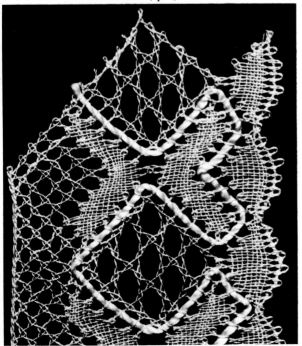

Setting-up diagram

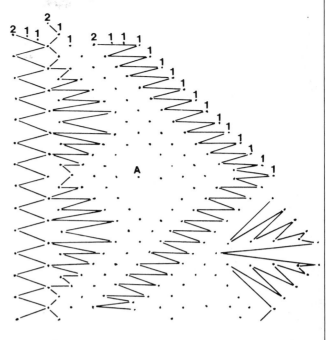

Materials:
- 25 pairs of bobbins.
- Thread no. 80.

Working method:
- Hang the bobbins on the pins in accordance with the setting-up diagram.
- Stitches used:
  - whole stitch
  - whole stitch and twist
  - half stitch, pin, half stitch
  - open spider (see detail)

Detail A
Open spider

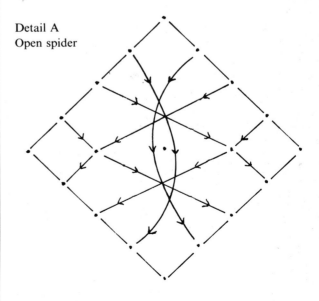

Materials:
- 22 pairs of bobbins, thread no. 70.
- 1 pair of bobbins with a gimp thread.

Working method:
- Hang on the pairs as shown in the setting-up diagram.
  On pin D hang the gimp pair.
- This circular edging is worked in bucks point and whole stitch.
- Work the heading as indicated by the lines.
- If you prefer a stronger headside, add another pair, which is worked along the edge in whole stitch and twist, no pin.

Setting-up diagram

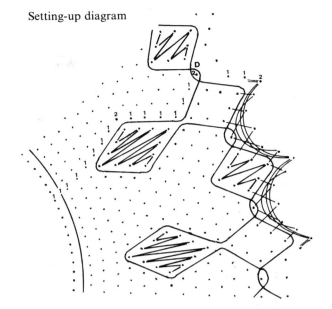

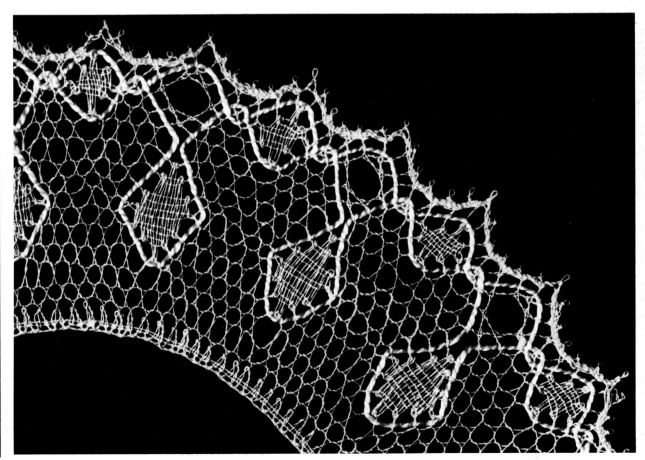

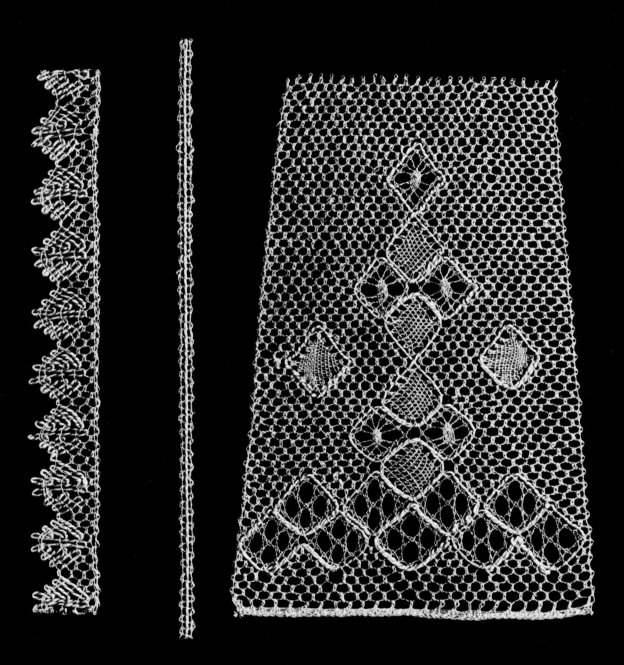

The three separate parts of this design together form a shade for a table lamp, which fits to a frame with a top diameter of about 10 cm (4 in) and a bottom diameter of about 13 cm (5 in). These frames are sold by most craft suppliers.

Part 1 is the covering of the shade and must be made × 4. Afterwards, it is attached to the bars of the frame.

Part 2 is a decorative braid to be fastened to the vertical bars of the frame after attaching part 1 to it. Four of these braids, each of about 17 cm (7 in) in length, are needed. Finishing the upper edge of the shade requires about 32 cm (12½ in).

Part 3 is a decorative edging, to be attached to the lower edge of the shade. This requires about 42 cm (16½ in) of lace.

Part 1

Materials:
- 58 pairs of bobbins with thread no. 80.
- 5 pairs of bobbins with a gimp.

Working method:
- At each pinhole between the letters A and B (see pricking) 2 pairs of bobbins are hung.
- Start at A. The outer pairs are worked in whole stitch and twist. The net is worked in torchon double ground throughout (whole stitch and twist, pin, whole stitch and twist). Emphasise all motifs with a gimp. These pairs are hung at the pinholes marked D in the pricking.
  The motifs are made of spiders, half stitch, whole stitch and honeycomb.
- The bottom selvedge is worked 4 rows of whole stitch. Next whole stitch × 4 and take the worker out of the working area by putting it upwards on the lace. Start again with the first pair, whole stitch × 4 and upwards on the lace again. Start first pair again, etc. The bobbins can be cut off close to the work afterwards.

Part 2

This braid is worked with 3 pairs of bobbins with thread no. 80 and 1 bobbin with a gimp, hung at D. Work whole stitch and twist throughout; the gimp is worked between the stitches.

Part 3

For the edging made of fans 8 pairs of bobbins, thread no. 80 and 1 bobbin with a gimp are required. For the hanging of the pairs see the pricking. Along the footside whole stitch and twist, fill with torchon double ground and work the fan with the gimp as worker.

Materials:
- 43 pairs of bobbins, thread no. 70.
- 1 pair of bobbins with a gimp thread.

Working method:
- At each pinhole on the line A-B 1 pair of bobbins is hung, with the exception of A, where 2 pairs are hung.
  Hang the gimp pair at D.
- Start the work at A and finish the triangle A-B-C completely (see pricking).
- Next turn the pillow so that A is on the top left hand corner and start anew at C.
- The smaller triangles are worked in triangular ground.

Setting-up diagram

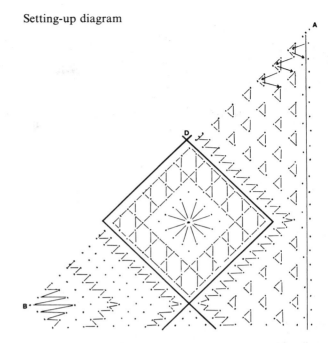

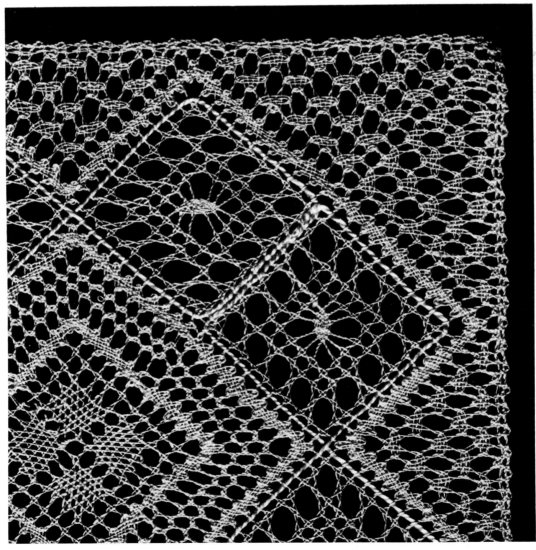

This design consists of an outer edge and an inner circle.

1 Outer edge

Materials:
– 36 pairs of bobbins, thread no. 70.
– 1 pair of bobbins with a gimp.

Working method:
– Hang on the pairs as shown in setting-up diagram no. 1.
– The edge is worked in whole stitch, half stitch, torchon ground and footside stitch.
– At A: 2 pairs of bobbins whole stitch and twist.
– At B: 2 pairs of bobbins whole stitch.
– Take C and D out of the ground in whole stitch at E.
– At G: leave 2 pairs, which will re-enter the ground.
– To H, whole stitch × 3, whole stitch and twist, pin and back to J.
– Repeat this process continuously.
– The passives K and L are worked in whole stitch, between the stitches of the ground. The outer pair are whole stitch and twist.

Setting-up diagram no. 1

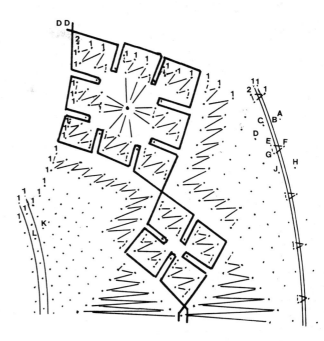

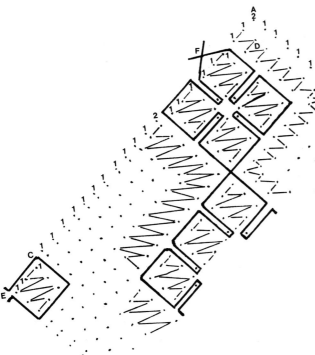

2 Inner Circle

Materials:
– 33 pairs of bobbins, thread no. 70. (Now and again you may have to add a number of bobbins in working this lace).
– 1 pair of bobbins with a gimp.
– 1 single bobbin with a gimp.

Working method:
– Hang on the bobbins as shown in setting-up diagram no. 2.
  The single gimp thread is hung at E, the gimp pair at F.
– Hang on the pairs on the line A-B in the outer edge.
– At C bring a pair into the whole stitch diamond.
– Braid D is worked in bias ground.
– Work the first quarter of the pattern, then turn the pillow and work the next quarter.

Setting-up diagram no. 2

Setting-up diagram

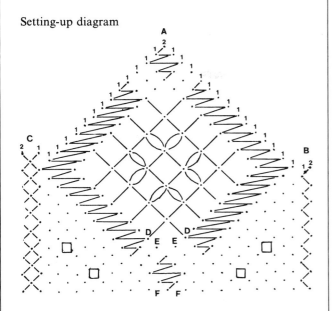

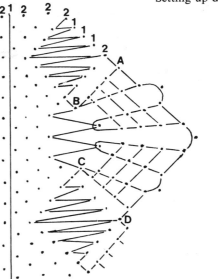

Materials:
— 35 pairs of bobbins.
— Thread no. 50.

Working method:
— Start at A; work the diamond in whole stitch.
— Continue hanging the pairs as shown above.
— At B: 2 pairs whole stitch and twist and 1 pair whole stitch for the heading.
— At C: whole stitch and twist × 3 for the footside.
— Leave out 2 pairs at D. These pairs are worked into the ground at E.
— Pick up 2 pairs from the ground at F.

Materials:
— 14 pairs of bobbins.
— Thread no. 100.

Working method:
— Hang on the pairs as indicated by the setting-up diagram.
— Start at A with the fan.
— At B work 3 pairs into whole stitch bar.
— At C leave out 3 pairs.
— At D use 2 passive pairs.
— Stitches used:
  ● footside stitch
  ● torchon ground
  ● whole stitch for the diamond
  ● torchon double ground for the fan.

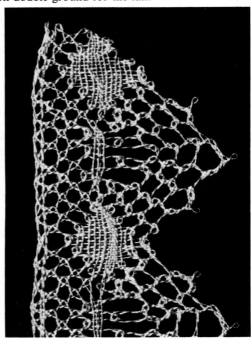

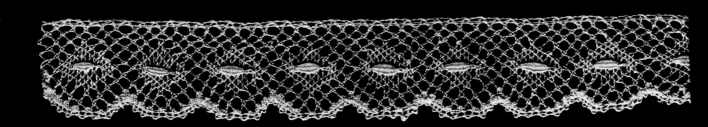

Pattern 26

Setting-up diagram

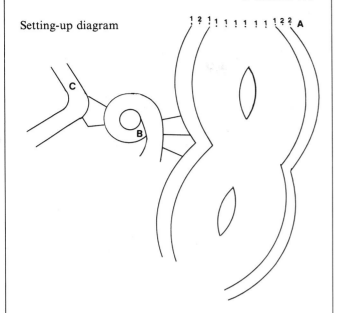

Materials:
- 15 pairs of bobbins for the outer edge.
- 5 pairs of bobbins for the braids in the inner oval.
- Thread no. 100.

Working method:
- Hang on the bobbins in accordance with the setting-up diagram.
- Start at A, whole stitch and twist, whole stitch × 2 and half stitch as far as the last three pairs. They are worked whole stitch × 2 and whole stitch and twist.
- Make the leaf with the 7th and 8th pair.
- At B 5 pairs of bobbins are hung for the braid. Sew the braid to the outer edge with the worker.
- Hang 5 pairs at C.
- The leaves in the middle of the mat are worked last.

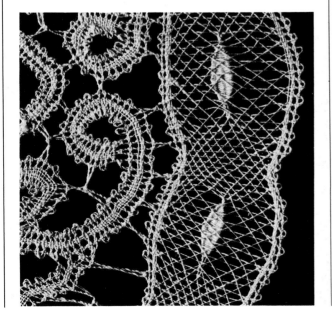

Pattern 27

Setting-up diagram

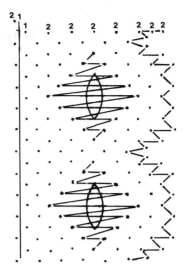

Materials:
- 18 pairs of bobbins.
- Thread no. 70.

Working method:
- Start as shown in the setting-up diagram.
- After reaching the leaf in the half stitch diamond, this is to be worked first with the 2 middle pairs. Put up a pin and continue the diamond as far as the bottom of the leaf. The 2 leaf pairs re-enter the half stitch diamond. Finish the diamond.
- Note: the leaves are *under* the half stitch diamond while working!

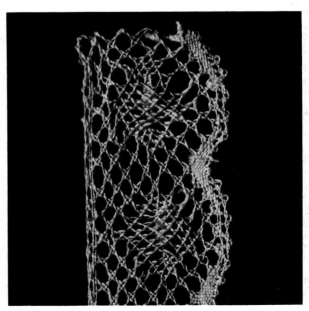

This instruction actually describes 2 separate mats, viz.
- the outer edge and
- the inner circle (which can also be used as a smaller separate mat, without the outer edge).

1 Outer Edge

Materials:
- 18 pairs of bobbins.
- Thread no. 50.

Working method:
- Hang on the bobbins as shown in the setting-up diagram.
- Start at A and work whole stitch and twist, whole stitch × 4 to B and back.
- Make a picot at C.
- From B make a plait (with or without picot), through D, E and F to G.
- At E make a double crossing. The pairs coming from the leaf should be in the middle.
- At H whole stitch and twist.
- At J whole stitch and twist with picot.
- At K whole stitch and twist.
- At G the pairs of the plait are taken into the whole stitch bar.

Setting-up diagram

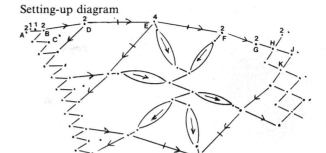

2 Inner Circle

Materials:
- 18 pairs of bobbins.
- Thread no. 50.

Working method:
- Look at the pricking for the hanging of the pairs.
- Start hanging 12 pairs of bobbins at the small numbers in the pattern.
- Work as the arrows indicate.
- Finish this circle.
- Then hang 6 pairs of bobbins at the pinholes marked with large numbers.
- These pairs work the centre flower.

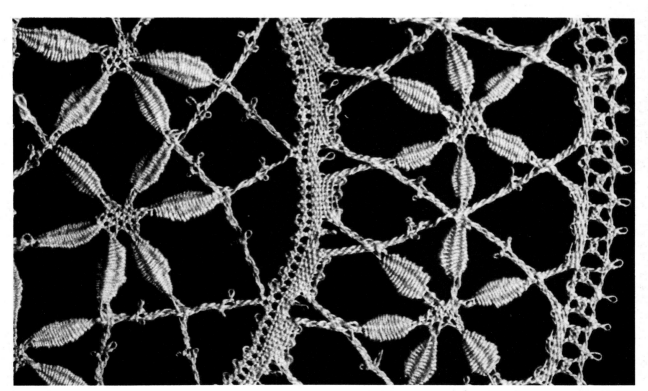

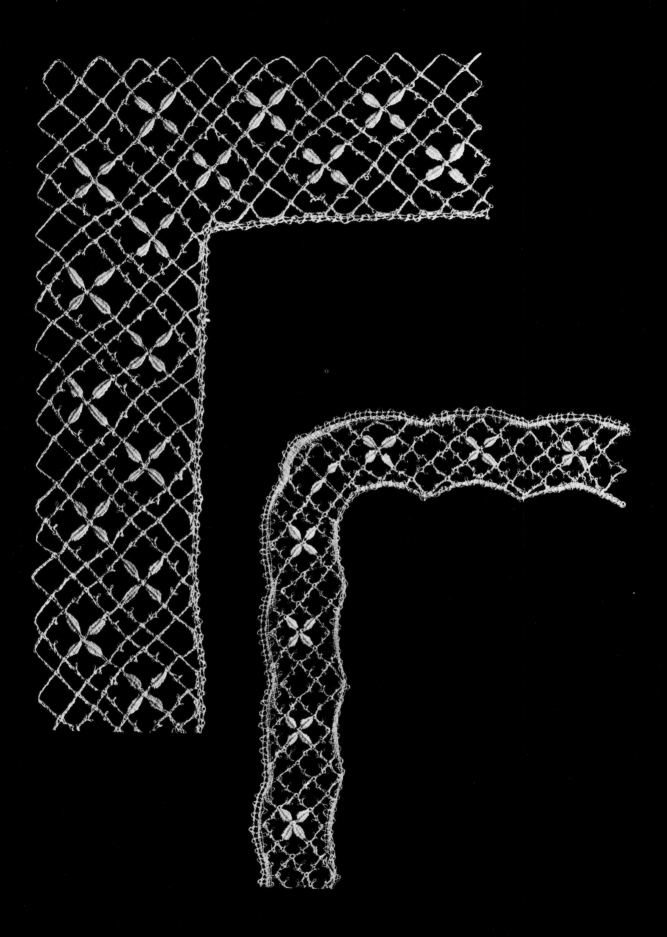

Setting-up diagram

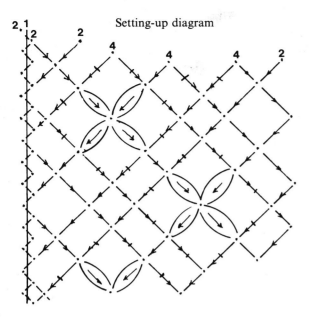

Setting-up diagram

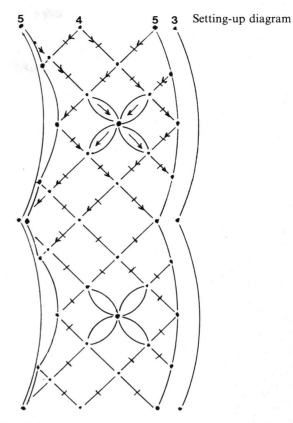

Materials:
— 21 pairs of bobbins.
— Thread no. 70.

Working method:
— Hang the bobbins as shown in the setting-up diagram.
— Work footside stitch: whole stitch and twist, then whole stitch.
— This lace is worked in plaits with and without picots and leaves, in accordance with the arrows.

Materials:
— 17 pairs of bobbins.
— Thread no. 100.

Working method:
— Hang on the pairs as shown in the setting-up diagram.
— Work in the direction indicated by the arrows.
— Stitches used:
  ● whole stitch
  ● footside stitch
  ● plaits with picots
  ● leaves

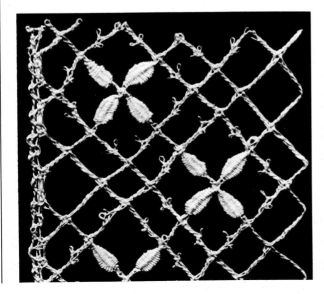

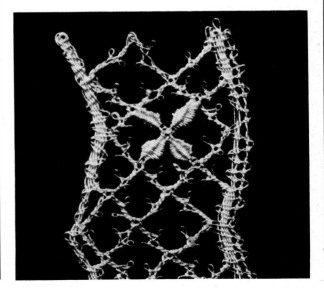

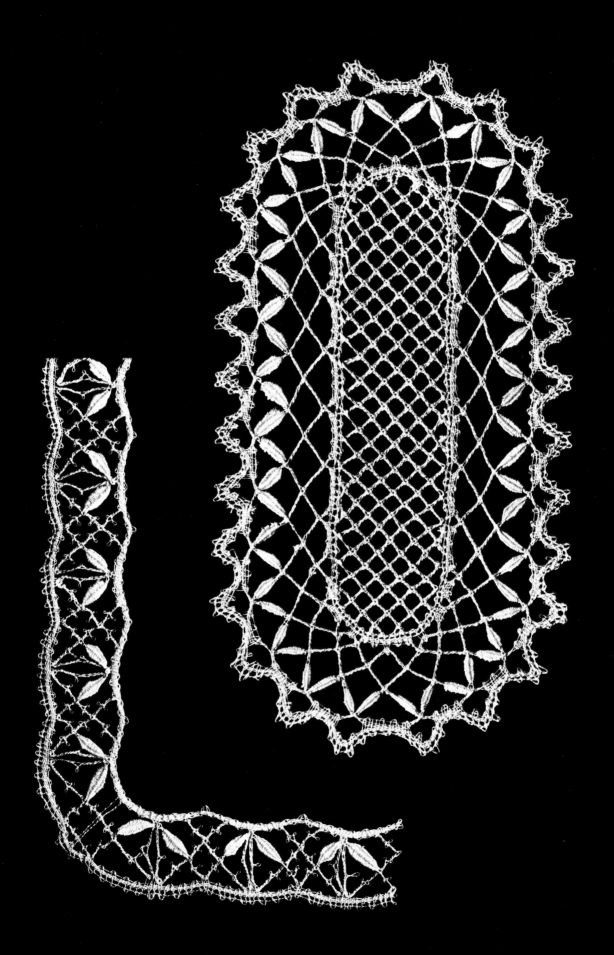

Pattern 31

Setting-up diagram

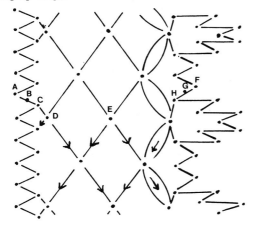

Materials:
- 17 pairs of bobbins for the outer edge.
- About 22 pairs of bobbins for the filling.
- Thread no. 70.

Working method:
- Start at A.
- Hang 2 pairs at A, 1 pair at B and 2 pairs at C.
- Work these pairs in whole stitch and twist, then whole stitch × 3, pin, and back.
- Hang 2 pairs at D.
- Make a plait from C to D and continue in the direction indicated by the arrows.
- Hang 4 pairs at E. Again proceed as shown by the arrows, 2 pairs to the left, 2 pairs to the right as far as the leaf.
- Hang 2 pairs on each of the pins F, G and H.
  With these pairs work whole stitch and twist first, then whole stitch × 4, pin and back.
- At H make a plait towards the leaf, cross with the pairs coming from E and make the leaf.
- Continuously repeat the procedure as described above.
- The filling is worked in plaits.

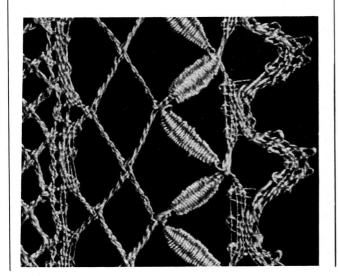

Pattern 32

Setting-up diagram

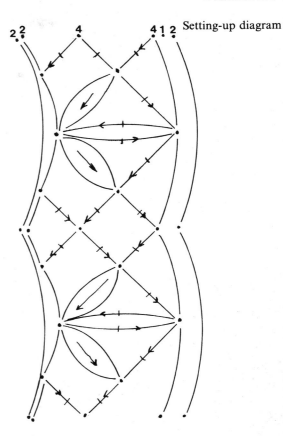

Materials:
- 15 pairs of bobbins.
- Thread no. 80.

Working method:
- Hang on the pairs as shown in the setting-up diagram.
- Work the plaits, picots and leaves in accordance with the arrows.
- In the corner pass the worker through the plaits from footside to heading, join with outside edge and return to footside (see pricking).

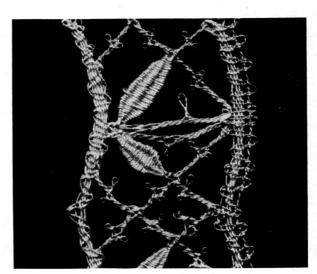

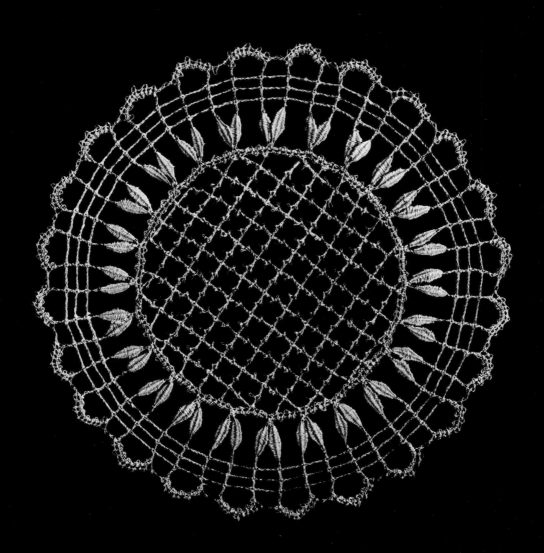

Materials:
— 14 pairs of bobbins.
— Thread no. 90.

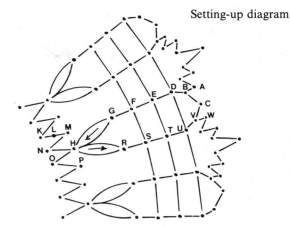

Working method:
— Hang 2 pairs at A and make a whole stitch and twist.
— Hang 2 pairs at B. Make a whole stitch with left hand pair, using the pairs at B and whole stitch × 2, whole stitch and twist to C.
— Hang 2 pairs round each of the pins D, E and F.
— From B make a plait passing through D-E-F. Plait to G and make a leaf to H.
— Hang 2 pairs at K and 1 pair at L and M. From K whole stitch and twist, whole stitch × 2 to M, pin and back to N.
— Next to H; bring the worker through the leaf pairs and back to O, then continue to P, etc.
— At H make a leaf to R, plait through S-T-U to V.
— With the left hand pair of the plait whole stitch × 2, whole stitch and twist and to W (using the pairs at C).
— In this way complete the curve.
— Repeat this procedure continuously.
— The filling in the centre requires about 30 pairs of bobbins.
— Work plaits with picots.

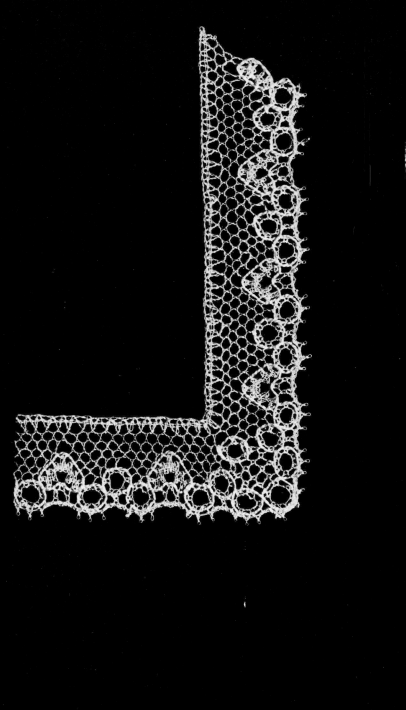
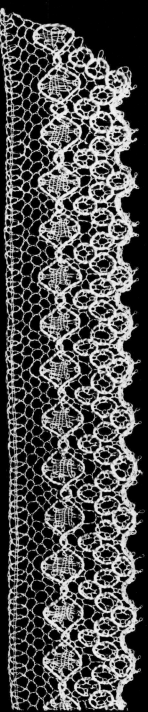

Setting-up diagram no. 1

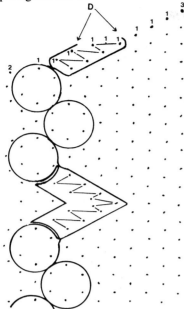

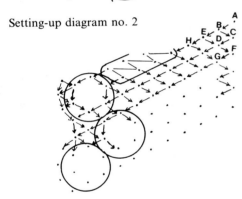

Setting-up diagram no. 2

Materials:
- 14 pairs of bobbins, thread no. 70.
- 1 pair of bobbins with a gimp.

Working method:
- Hang on the pairs as shown in setting-up diagram no. 1. The gimp is hung at D.
- Now look at setting-up diagram no. 2.
- At A: whole stitch and twist, whole stitch, pin at pinhole B, where 1 pair is already hanging.
- With this pair Bucks point stitch, *no* pin, whole stitch, whole stitch and twist and put a pin between 2nd and 3rd pair at C, in this case counting from the *right!*
- At C: 2nd pair whole stitch, double twist and put a pin at D.
- At E work to D, Bucks point stitch, no pin, continue the footside as described above, and put a pin at F.
- From F to G, put a pin and work the pair from H to G. Make the footside, etc.
- The heart is worked in whole stitch. The six pin ring in honeycomb stitch. The headside is whole stitch with picot.

Setting-up diagram no. 1

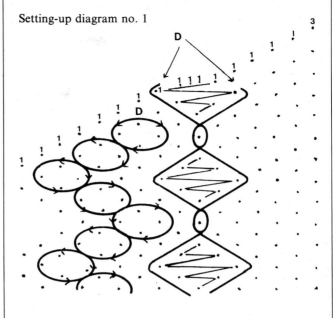

Setting-up diagram no. 2

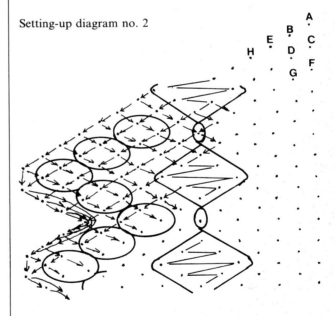

Materials:
- 19 pairs of bobbins, thread no. 80.
- 2 pairs of bobbins with a gimp.

Working method:
- Hang on the pairs in accordance with setting-up diagram no. 1. The gimp pairs are hung at D.
- Now look at setting-up diagram no. 2.
- Work as shown in the 2nd setting-up diagram of pattern 34.
- Work the diamond in whole stitch.
- The four pin rings are worked in honeycomb stitch.
- The heading is whole stitch with picot. Work as the arrows indicate.

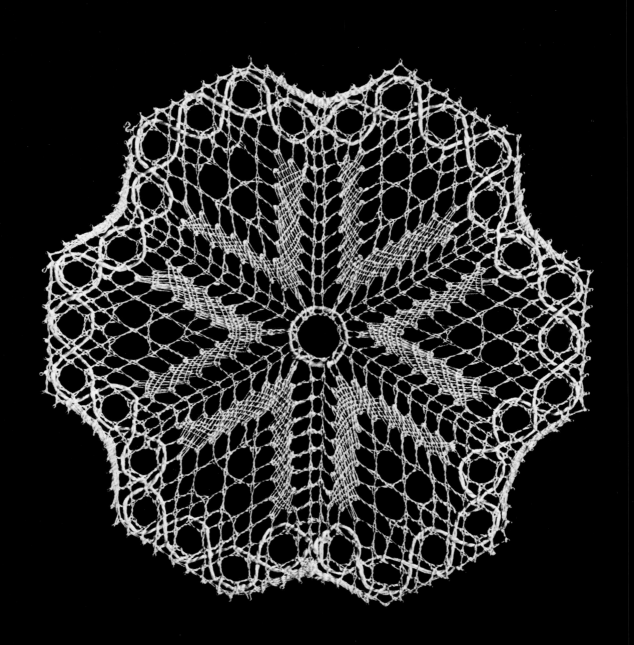

Setting-up diagram

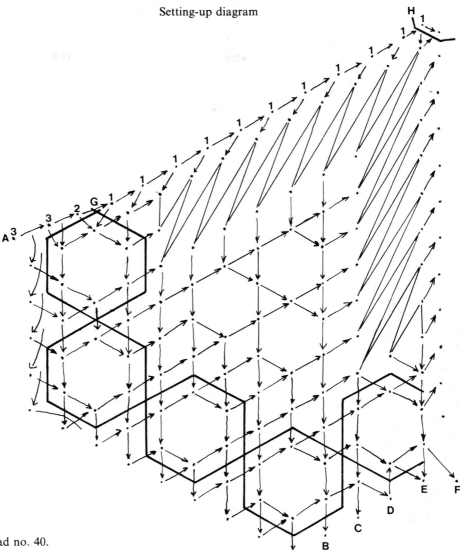

Materials:
— 19 pairs of bobbins with thread no. 40.
— 1 pair of bobbins with a gimp.
— 1 single bobbin with a gimp.

Working method:
— Hang on the bobbins as shown in the setting-up diagram. The gimp pair is hung at G and the single bobbin with the gimp thread at H.
— At A work whole stitch × 7, pass through gimp and from there on half stitch, pin, half stitch with an extra twist as far as centre ring. Hang the single bobbin with the gimp just before the last pair.
— 6th pair, whole stitch × 5, picot and back through 4 pairs, no pin.
— 6th and 7th pair enter honeycomb ring.
— 5th pair works to the left, whole stitch × 4, picot, whole stitch × 4; this pair enters the honeycomb ring too.
— 4th pair, to the left, whole stitch × 3, picot, whole stitch × 3, half stitch, pin, half stitch with 5th pair.
— 5th pair enters honeycomb ring.
— Take 4th pair, to the left, whole stitch × 3, picot, whole stitch × 2.

— Now finish the honeycomb ring, etc., following the arrows.
— Continue the headside with the 3rd and 4th pair; work into honeycomb ring.
— 2nd pair whole stitch, picot and back into honeycomb.
— 1st pair makes picot, whole stitch with 2nd pair.
— 2nd pair makes picot and whole stitch, enters honeycomb ring, and leaves again to make picot, whole stitch, etc.
— Continue as shown by the arrows.
— At B with 3rd pair whole stitch × 2, picot, whole stitch × 2, no pin.
— At C with 4th pair whole stitch × 2, picot, whole stitch × 3, no pin.
— With 5th pair to D, whole stitch × 4, picot, whole stitch × 4, no pin.
— With 6th pair to E, whole stitch × 5, picot.
— With 7th pair to F, whole stitch × 6, etc.
— Start again at F; look at the description at A.

Materials:
— 21 pairs of bobbins.
— Thread no. 50 or 60.

Working method:
— Start at A with 4 pairs of bobbins in whole stitch × 2
    — whole stitch and twist.
— At B and C: hang 2 × 3 pairs for the spider.
— Hang 1 pair at each of the pinholes D, E and F.
  They are used for the braid in the motif.
— At H: hang 2 pairs of bobbins, of which one is
  worked as a passive pair in the footside. The other is
  used as worker in the motif.
— At K and L: hang 1 pair for the spider. The 3rd leg
  of the spider is picked up from the braid.
— Hang 1 pair at each of the pinholes M, N and P.
— Continue as indicated by the arrows.

Setting-up diagram

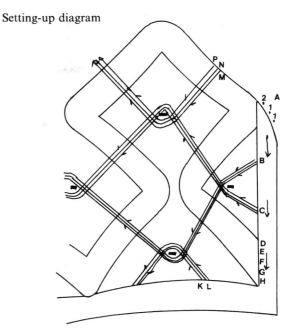

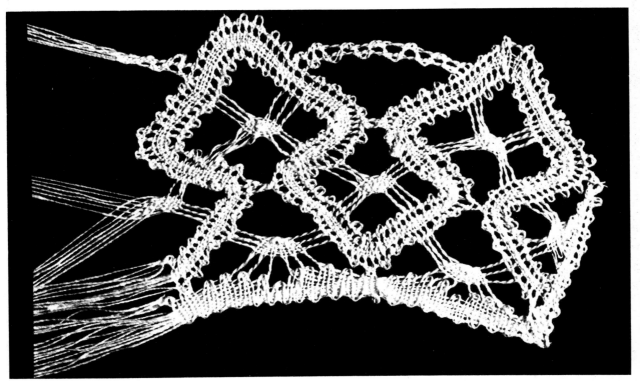

Note:
The right hand side of the pricking is illustrated on the next page. Place the asterisks on top of each other to make the pricking complete.

Pricking 3

Pricking 2
right side

Pricking 4

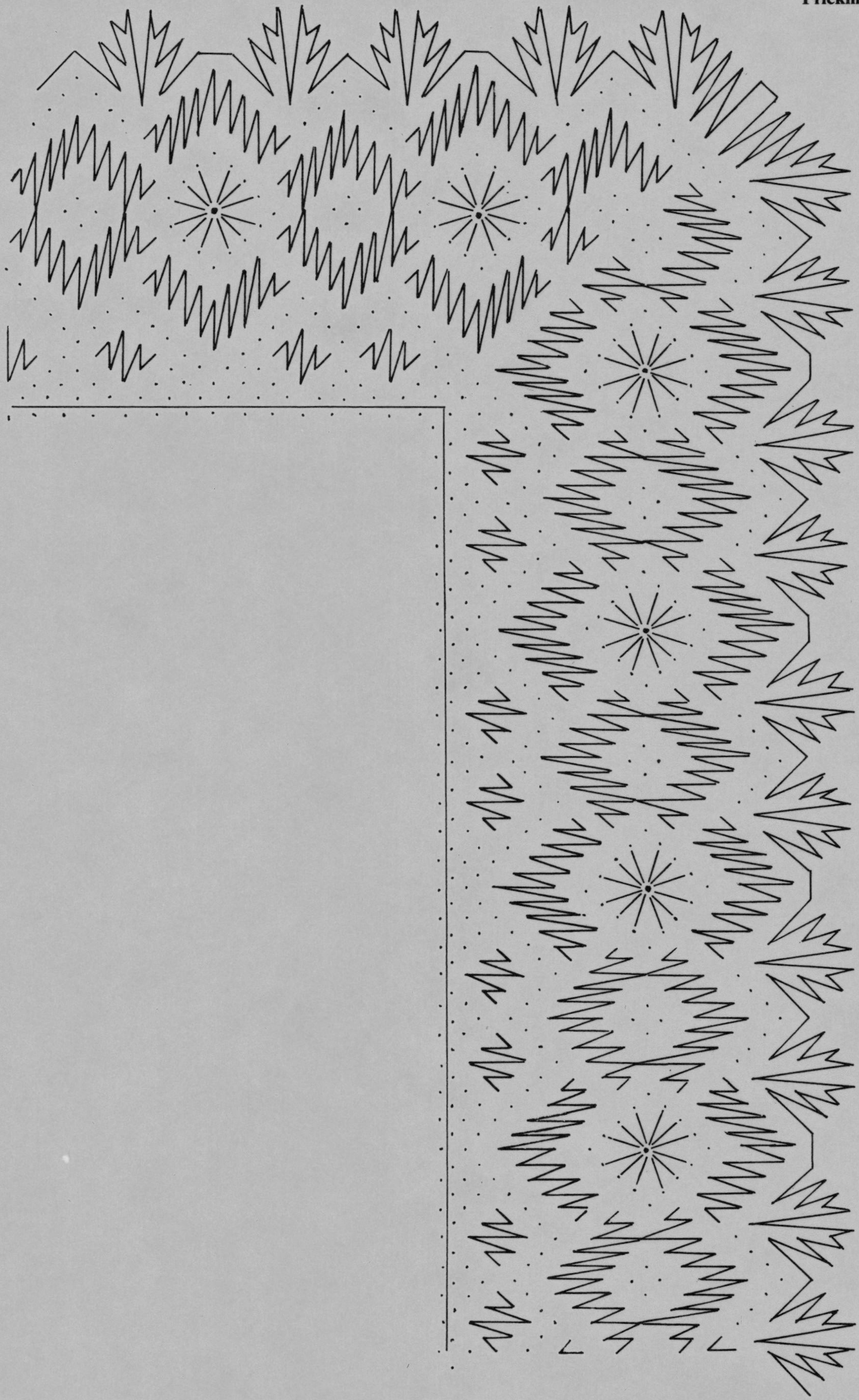

*

*

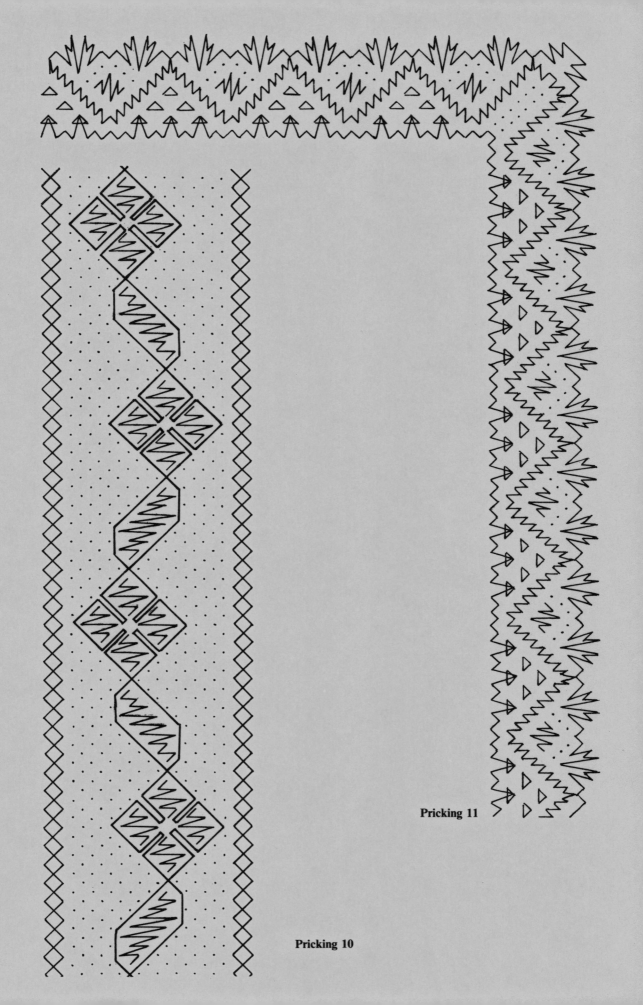

Pricking 11

Pricking 10

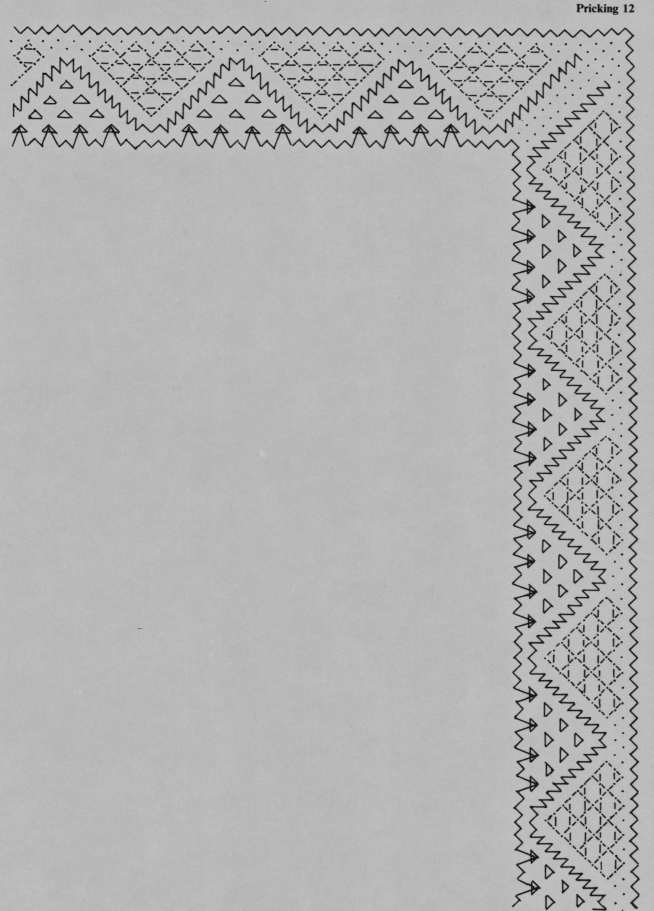

Pricking 20
right side

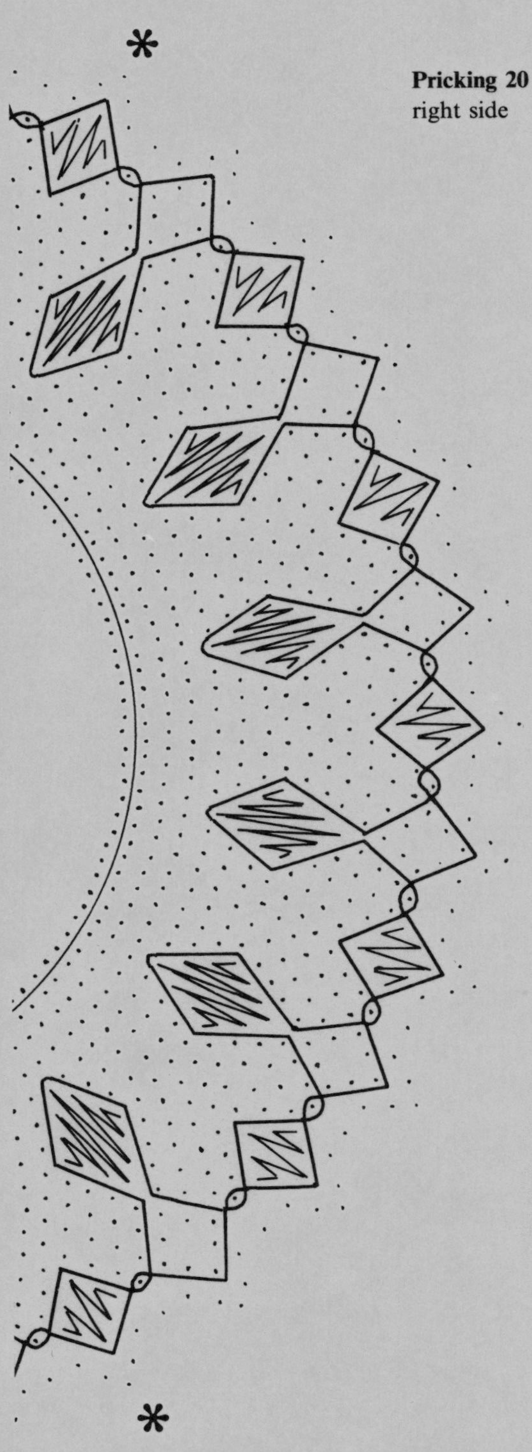

*

Pricking 19

*

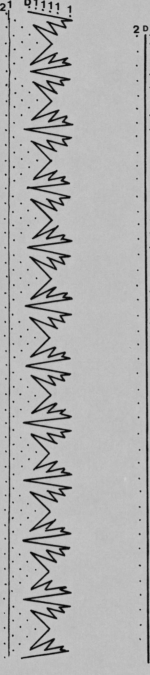

part 3

part 2

part 1

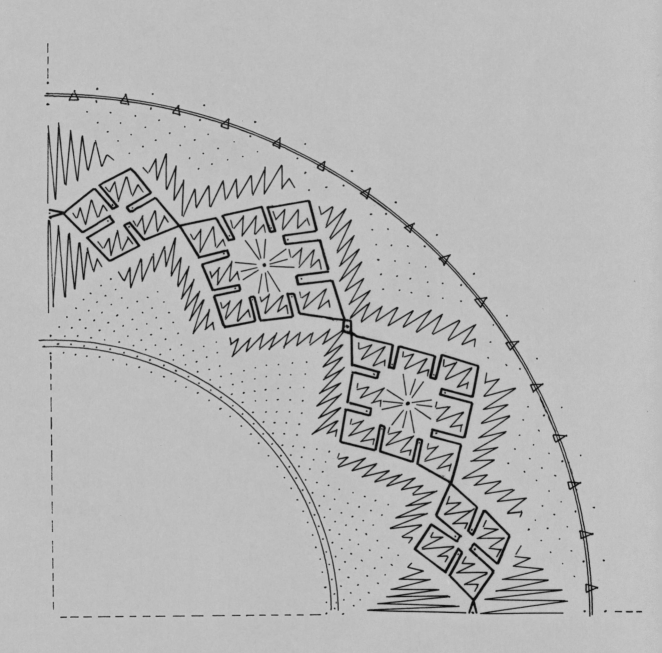

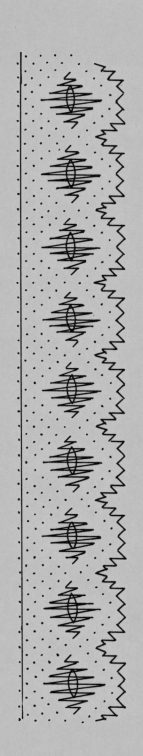

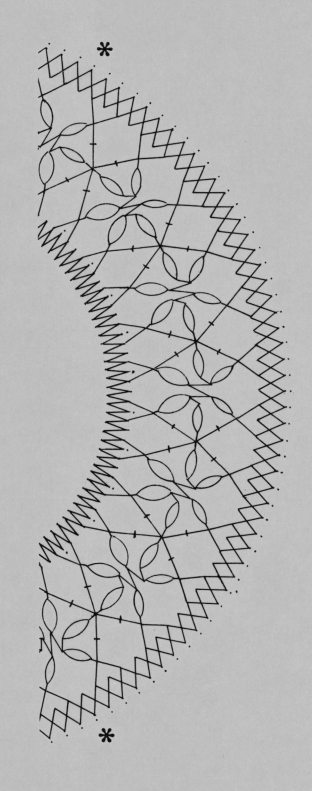

*

*

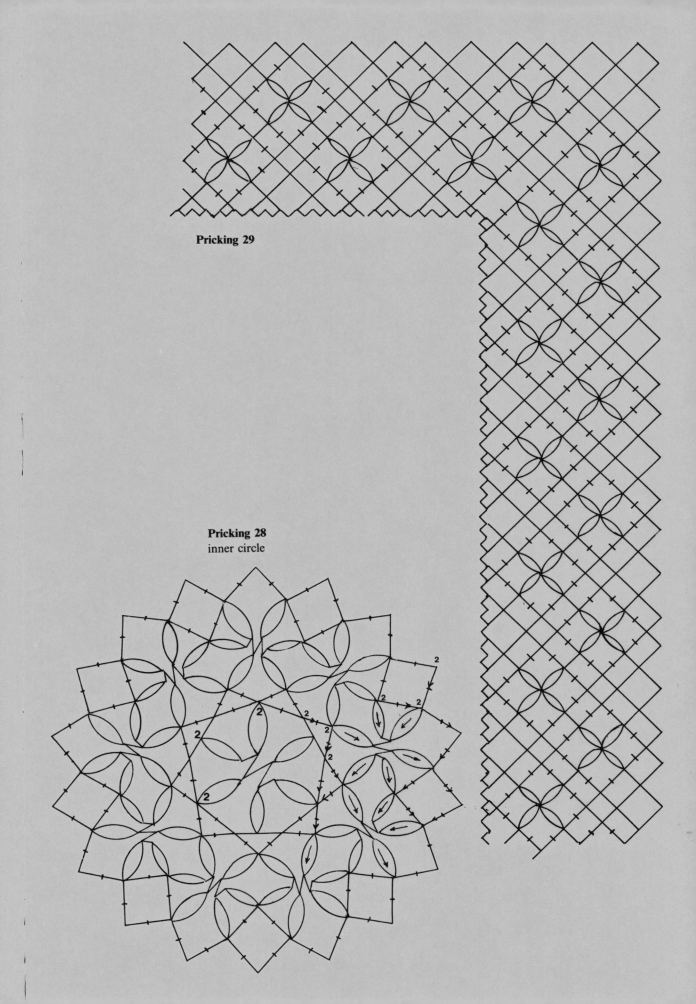

Pricking 29

Pricking 28
inner circle

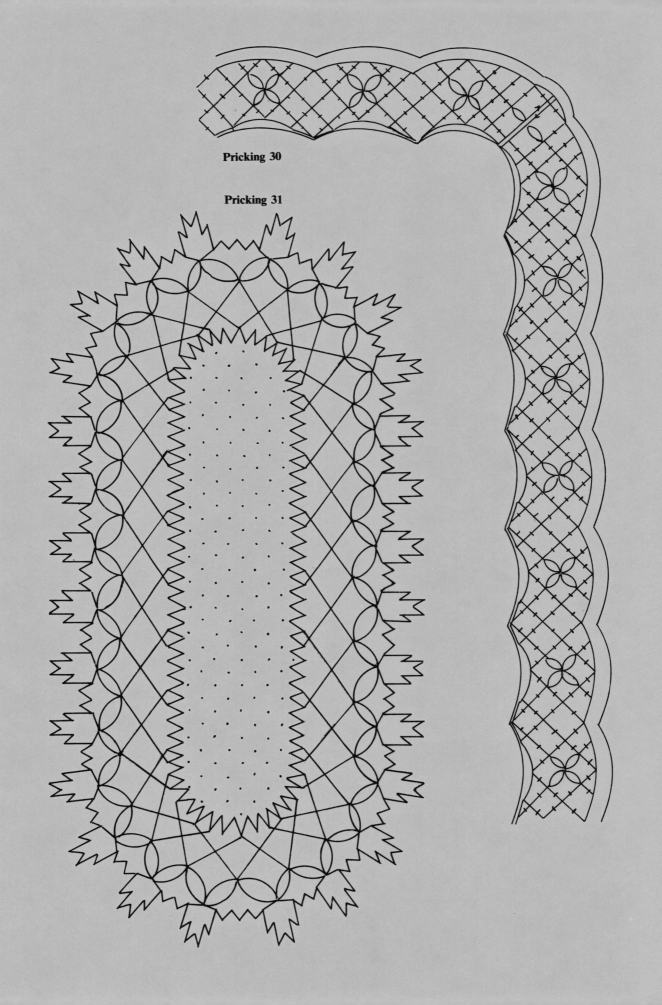

Pricking 30

Pricking 31

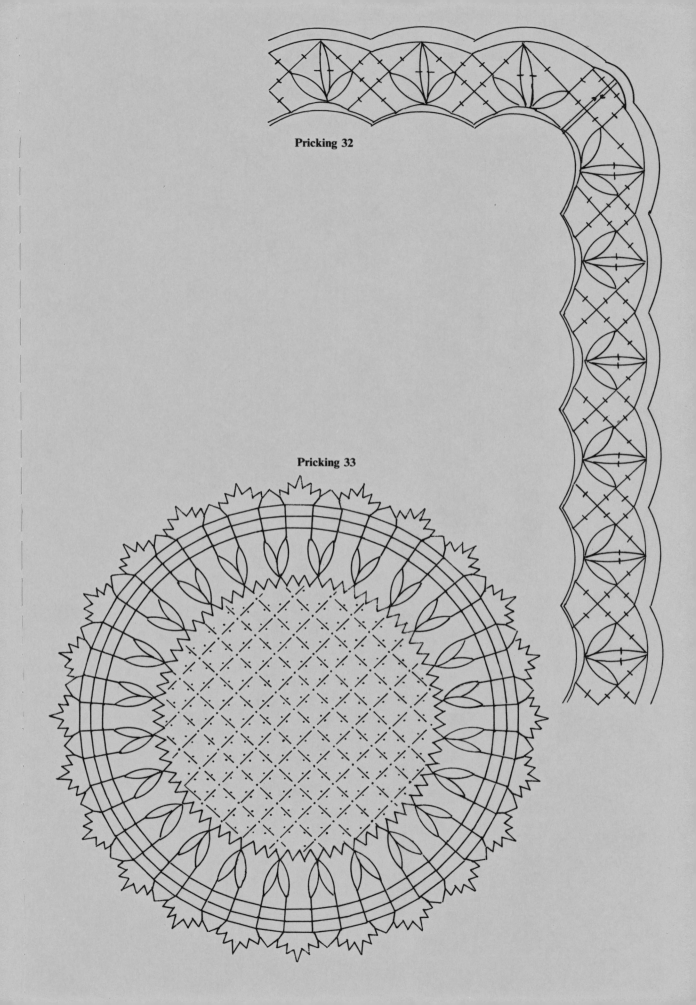

Pricking 32

Pricking 33

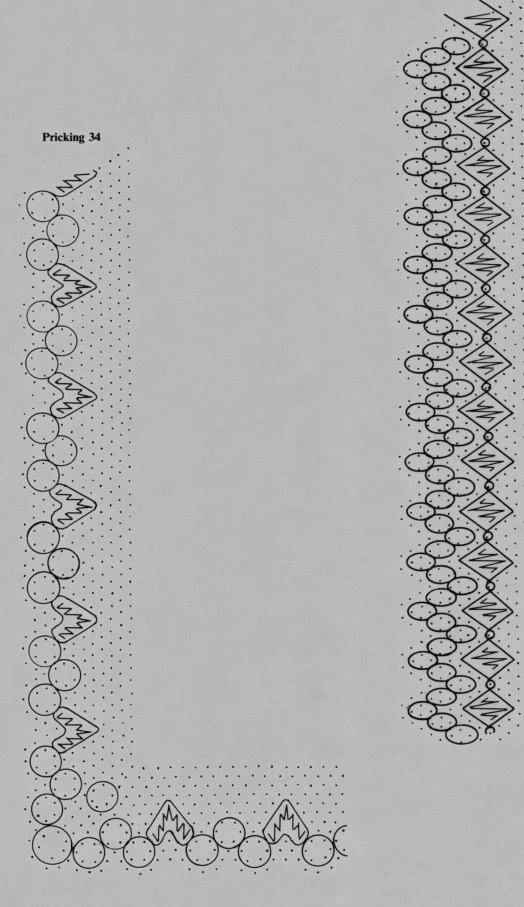

Pricking 35

Pricking 34

Note:
Joining the two halves of the pricking at the V-V line will
give you a collar for an adult. Joining at the T-T line,
however, will make the collar suitable for a teenager.